AF433599

Table of Contents

Introduction

Soil building is a plant driven process whereby carbon is sequestered from the atmosphere and locked into the soil and in so doing, changes the overall biological, chemical and physical properties of the soil – in a beneficial way.

Soil organic matter can be divided into 3 parts – the living, the dead and the very dead.

The living part – huge diversity of micro-organisms, such as bacteria, viruses, fungi, protozoa, algae and nematodes; also, plant roots, insects, earthworms, and larger animals.

The dead part – dead plant roots, crop residues, root exudates, deceased micro and macro organisms, and animal manures. This is the active, or easily decomposed, fraction of organic matter that is the main supply of food for the various organisms.

The very dead part – humus – very stable, complex and well-decomposed organic matter. Humus is an organo-mineral complex comprising about 60% carbon and between 6 and 8% nitrogen, phosphorus and sulphur.

Proportionally, it has a huge surface area and can store both cations and anions and is an essential factor in soil fertility. These organo-mineral complexes form a stable and inseparable part of the soil matrix that can remain intact for hundreds of years.

The ultimate goal in soil building is the formation of humus.

There are 2 pathways whereby humus can be formed and they differ substantially in their effectiveness.

1. Pathway One is the decomposition of organic materials such as – crop residues and manures

To obtain the energy contained in cellulose, lignin, starches, oils or other compounds formed by plants, microbes have to break this material down. This is called mineralisation. In so doing, between 60 and 80% of this carbon is released as CO_2 back to the atmosphere through a process called oxidation and respiration. The efficiency of this process is determined by the digestibility of the material, the microbial community present, soil moisture content and other environmental conditions.

The type of vegetation also has a major impact on the amount of carbon sequestration. In forest soils, most of the soil organic matter (SOM) is distributed in the top few centimetres, mostly as a result of leaf litter. Tree roots are high in lignin and do not die off on a regular basis and thus do not contribute much to SOM. In comparison, tall grasses form deep fibrous root systems of which 50% die off yearly. Their decomposition happens at depth and thus these soils are high in SOM throughout the soil profile making them highly productive because they hold more nutrients, contain more microbes, and have better soil structure due to larger fungal populations.

2. Pathway Two is liquid carbon exudates resynthesised into highly complex carbon polymers

The carbon found at the soil surface are mostly short-chain, labile (easily altered, less stable) carbon, indicative of rapid turnover. This is the active carbon that is important for the health of the soil food-web. In recent scientific studies it was found that on average only 8,3% of this carbon was converted to stable soil humus.

The carbon in root exudates is already in a useable form for microbes. Very little carbon loss occurs through respiration (CO2 release) and virtually no losses occur through oxidation. The same study found that on average 46% of root-derived carbon was stabilised making this pathway 5 times more efficient than the Pathway One alternative involving ground biomass. The liquid carbon pathway allows for carbon sequestration deeper down in the soil profile, building top soil at depth, so to speak. The deeper the sequestration, the greater the likelihood that the carbon will be protected from oxidative and/or microbial decomposition.

TWO PATHWAYS OF CARBON SEQUESTRATION

Every green plant is in effect a solar-powered carbon pump and it is the photosynthetic capacity and the photosynthetic rate of plants that drives the sequestration of stable soil carbon. If plants are force fed with inorganic fertilisers, it shuts off this pump. Reduced carbon flows consequently impact a vast network of microbial communities, restricting the availability of essential minerals, trace elements, vitamins and hormones required for plant tolerance to environmental stresses such as frost, drought and resistance to insects and disease. Decreased nutrient densities in plants also translate to reduced nutritional value of food – a deadly and futile downward spiral of soil degradation.

PRACTICAL IMPLICATIONS

The use of inorganic fertilisers can be minimised by using it in conjunction with organic fertilisers, organic acids and Compost Tea. This will prevent the shut down of the carbon pump and will counter the oxidation of soil carbon.

Living plants are at least 5 times more efficient at building soil carbon than the decomposition of mulches. It is the photosynthetic capacity and the photosynthetic rate of plants that determines the effectiveness of the process.

Photosynthetic capacity is the amount of light intercepted in a given area. This can be optimised through the use of multi-species crops, stacking different height plants together. For instance, in fruit orchards diverse under-storey cover crops or weeds can be utilised to increase light interception and thus root exudates. Bare soil has zero photosynthetic capacity, is detrimental to soil health and should be avoided at all costs. The more active green leaves there are and the more roots there are, the more carbon is added.

With pastures it is recommended that stock be bunched into large mobs and moved frequently. During the grazing period (usually one to three days), a useful guide is to aim for approximately 20% of the available forage to be trampled to form surface litter and approximately 20% to be left standing (ie. no more than 60% utilised for animal consumption). This will prevent that palatable forage is overgrazed and will ensure that enough photosynthetic capacity remains for regrowth.

Treating fruit trees with Ecosoil's Compost Tea will make them more complex, resulting in more shoots but shorter and more productive trees. Since the overall growth is more, this will increase the photosynthetic capacity.

Photosynthetic rate is the rate at which plants are able to convert light energy into sugars. There are many factors playing a role here – light intensity, temperature, moisture, nutrient availability, plant health, as well as microbial communities around roots and on leaf surfaces. Photosynthetic rate can be assessed by measuring sugar (Brix) levels with a refractometer. Diverse microbial communities perform soil functions that increase the photosynthetic rate of plants, increasing their mineral and sugar content and making them less prone to pest and disease. This in turn allows for more liquid carbon exudates, that in turn improves soil fertility and offers an upward spiral of soil regeneration.

NUTRIENT MANAGEMENT

Most of the 'deficiencies' observed in today's plants, animals and people are due to soil conditions not being conducive to nutrient uptake. The minerals are present, but simply not plant available. Adding inorganic elements to correct these so-called deficiencies is an inefficient practice. Rather, the biological causes of dysfunction must be addressed.

Soil aggregates are a fundamental unit of soil function

Soil aggregates are soil particles glued together into larger structures by micro-organisms. A great deal of biological activity takes place within aggregates. For the most part, this is fuelled by liquid carbon.

Most aggregates are connected to plant roots, often to very fine feeder roots, or to mycorrhizal networks unable to be detected with the naked eye. Mycorrhizal fungi, which form symbiotic relationships with plants are totally dependant on liquid carbon from green plants. They trade this carbon with colonies of bacteria located at their hyphal tips in exchange for macro-nutrients such as phosphorus, organic nitrogen and calcium, trace elements such as zinc, boron and copper, and plant growth stimulating substances. Mycorrhizal fungi then trade these nutrients for more liquid carbon from the plant.

Liquid carbon streams into the aggregates via these roots and fungal linkages, enabling the production of glues and gums by micro-organisms that hold soil particles together. These glues make the soil aggregates very stable against soil erosion.

Macroaggregates are essential to soil tilth, structure, aeration, infiltration, water-holding capacity, biological nitrogen fixation and carbon sequestration. In short, it is not possible to maintain healthy soils without them.

Nitrogen-fixing bacteria require a partial pressure difference in oxygen and water which is present between the inside and outside surface area of the aggregate. These conditions are essential to the functioning of the nitrogenase enzyme utilised for biological nitrogen fixation and also to the formation of humus.

As a result, nitrogen-fixing bacteria cannot function properly in compacted soils. Crops will not be able to obtain sufficient nitrogen and the tendency is then to add nitrogen fertiliser, exacerbating the downward spiral of soil degradation because it interrupts the carbon flow to soil, further reducing aggregation.

The chemical properties (minerals) of soil are also regulated by micro-organisms and facilitated by the production of humus

Humus contains about 60% carbon and between 6-8% nitrogen (N), phosphorus (P) and sulphur (S). Organic carbon, organic nitrogen and moisture holding capacity always move together. When soil carbon increases, so too do levels of organic nitrogen and the ability of the soil to infiltrate and store water. Soils become more fertile as a result. Higher organic matter content also buffers the soil against salt damage and pH fluctuations.

For every 1% organic matter, the soil can store 20 to 30 kg/ha of N and 4 to 7 kg/ha of P. Where soil was regenerated to contain 5% organic matter, it will be able to store 100 to 150 kg/ha of N and 20 to 35 kg/ha of P for free!

Amino forms of N are the most metabolically efficient form for plant uptake

In well-functioning soils, 85-90% of plant nutrient uptake is microbially mediated and N is no exception. The atmosphere contains 78% nitrogen. Biologically fixed ammonium (NH_4^+) and NH_4^+ derived from decomposition of organic matter is rapidly incorporated into organic molecules such as amino acids and humus in healthy soils.

NITROGEN CYCLE

Some of the inorganic forms of nitrogen derived from organic matter breakdown and from applied fertilisers are immobilised in the bodies of soil microbes. This prevents the leaching of these minerals. These are later cycled back into the system as organic nitrogen when they are consumed by other microbes, typically by protozoa, nematodes and other predators. Amino forms of N are the most metabolically efficient form for plant uptake. This pathway closes the nitrogen loop, reducing losses due to nitrification, denitrification, volatilisation and leaching. Additionally, the storage of nitrogen in the organic form prevents soil acidification.

Mineralisation of soil nutrients

Phosphorous is a major macronutrient needed by plants but is not easily taken up due to it's reactive nature with iron, aluminum, and calcium. These reactions result in the precipitation of phosphorous, thus making it unavailable to plants in the absence of microbial activity.

Some soil organisms in Ecosoil's Compost Tea can convert phosphorous into a more plant attainable form, such as orthophosphate. Iron is also another essential nutrient, but it is scarce in soil. Microbes can produce compounds called siderophores, which acquire ferric iron (Fe^{3+}), which plants can then take up.

Plant growth hormone production

Microbes found in Compost Tea can regulate plant growth promotion by the production of hormones and other compounds. Auxin is a class of plant hormones important in the promotion of lateral root formation. Increased lateral root formation leads to an enhanced ability to take up nutrients for the plant. Other classes of plant hormones include Gibberellins and Cytokinins, which both stimulate shoot development.

Hormone production and the uptake of N in organic farm can be the reason why we see better fruit colour development on trees treated with Ecosoil's Compost Tea.

Compost Tea organisms also have indirect effects on plant growth and thus fertiliser use

They degrade toxic substances that inhibit root growth, typically by-products from anaerobic bacteria and pesticide residues.

By reducing soil compaction, plants expend less energy on forcing roots through hard soil.

Our microbes increase stress tolerances against drought, pathogen attack, salinity and frost.

They increase the photosynthetic capacity and photosynthetic rate of plants.

The breakdown of organic matter is more efficient, creating stable humus that function as a bio-filter, preventing nutrients from leaching and improving water holding capacity.

They improve soil aeration allowing oxygen and nitrogen to enter which is crucial to root development and nitrogen fixation.

PRACTICAL IMPLICATIONS

The mineral cycle improves significantly when soils are alive. The sun's energy, captured in photosynthesis and channelled from above-ground to below-ground as liquid carbon via plant roots, fuels the microbes that solubilise the mineral fraction. A portion of the newly released minerals enable rapid humification in deep layers of soil, while the remaining minerals are returned to plant leaves, facilitating an elevated rate of photosynthesis and increased levels of production of liquid carbon, which in turn can be channelled to soil, enabling the dissolution of even more minerals.

The organisms in Compost Tea produce vitamins, plant growth hormones and enzymes which encourage strong root growth and release tied up nutrients. Many species of bacteria and fungi can access nutrients such as nitrogen and sulphur from the soil atmosphere, while others facilitate plant uptake of phosphorous, nitrogen and trace elements such as zinc, copper and molybdenum.

When bacteria proliferate, they require nitrogen and other minerals and temporally tie up these nutrients and so, indirectly prevent the leaching thereof. When plants require these nutrients, they signal protozoa species to proliferate and consume bacteria and to release the tied-up nutrients. These nutrients are in an organic form which plants prefer. Application of Compost Tea in conjunction with fertiliser programmes will save unutilised nutrients for the next season. So, typically fertiliser usage can be cut drastically from the second season onward.

WATER MANAGEMENT

Most parts of South Africa have experienced extended and unseasonal periods of drought these past few years. Climate variability is becoming an increasing problem. Most agricultural soils are not equipped to handle heavy down pours of rain, followed by long dry periods. Most soil surfaces are bare and capped, with little structural integrity. Rain drops hit bare soil with a tremendous force, dislodging soil particles and washing away valuable topsoil. This caps the soil, preventing water and air to infiltrate the soil.

Rivers in pristine areas, covered with vegetation and organic residues, are clear and fresh, compared to rivers running through agricultural areas which are brown with sediment and polluted with salts and nitrates. Crop residues play an important role in absorbing the force and reducing the damage that rain water can cause. Soil is never capped under organic residues. They slow down the surface flow of water, allowing more water to infiltrate the soil.

Water holding capacity

One part of humus can retain 4 parts of water. Soils with 3% carbon (approximately 6% organic matter) can store around 500 m3 of water per hectare, in addition to the water-holding capacity of the soil itself. As explained earlier, carbon sequestration through root derived carbon is 5 times more efficient than the breakdown of above ground organic residues. Therefore, year long green cover is the best way of building soil carbon levels and water storage capacity.

The use of Compost Tea in conjunction with other soil building practices will build soil carbon levels, improve water infiltration and water holding capacity. Many organisms in Compost Tea make plants more drought resistant. Besides producing chemical compounds that protect plants against desiccation, it also stimulates root branching and fine root development. Mycorrhizal fungi can supply moisture to plants in dry environments by exploring micropores not accessible to plant roots.

Secrets: 9 Ways to Improve Garden Soil

1. Feed it an Organic Diet

Spring brings a flurry of underground activity that we can't see. Billions of soil organisms stretch and yawn, exploding into existence. It's this living soil below ground that helps gardens thrive above ground by recycling nutrients, capturing water, improving soil tilth, and fighting pests and disease.

We build soil health all year-round by feeding and caring for it. How? Living soil has the same four basic requirements we do: food, water, shelter, and air.

Autumn is the best season to start. Organic materials, the key ingredients for healthy soils, abound. You can add fallen leaves, garden debris, kitchen scraps, and even apples raked from beneath fruit trees to soil.

Chop organic material directly into the top 2 inches of soil with a heavy bladed hoe and cover with mulch. Ideally, add concentrated manures, mineral phosphorous and potassium fertilizers, and lime at the same time. Adding these materials in the fall gives them time to break down for use when plants need them in the spring.

2. Till With Worms

Instead of breaking out the rototiller, or breaking my back double digging, I like to let the worms do my tilling for me by using sheet mulching techniques.

Sheet mulching is the process of building compost right on the soil surface. For new gardens, I'll add a smothering bottom layer of cardboard to kill existing vegetation, then alternate 2- to 4-inch-inch thick green and brown compost layers. This invites worms to burrow through the soil as they transport food. In the process, they dramatically improve soil structure, while depositing power-packed worm manure castings.

Sheet mulching takes advance planning. Ideally, start sheet mulches for new gardens the year before you plan to plant (and for existing gardens a few months before planting). Sheet mulching will build new garden soil literally from the ground up. It maximizes nutrients, smothers weeds, and keeps soil life intact and undisturbed.

3. Grow Your Own Soil

Green manures and cover crops—such as buckwheat and phacelia in the summertime and vetch, daikon, and clovers in the fall—are my favorite way to improve soils. Whenever I have a window before planting, I grow a cover crop to add organic matter, lighten and loosen soil structure, and enrich garden nutrients. Cover crops also act as a living mulch to shelter soils and control weeds in the off-season.

Chop over-wintered cover crops directly into spring soils a few weeks before planting. During the growing season, sow a quick-growing cover crop, such as buckwheat, to fill the gap between spring and fall crops. When it's time to plant, pull the buckwheat cover and use it as a mulch for fall garden beds.

4. Test for Success

Soil tests are an indispensable garden tool. I always recommend taking one when starting a new garden, or when garden health declines. If an essential nutrient is missing, garden and soil health will suffer. For best results, take nutrient tests in the late summer or early fall. Submit a soil test to a certified lab to add the right balance fertilizers and lime materials to new gardens.

5. Supply What's Missing

Over several seasons of soil building, a living, organic soil recycles and retains most nutrients, reducing or eliminating added fertilizer needs. When planting a new garden, however, organic fertilizers and lime ensure proper nutrition for the season ahead. If you've missed the fall window to add lime and mineral fertilizers, add them several weeks before planting in spring.

Use soil tests results and other resources to determine your garden's fertilizer needs. For general purposes, purchase a complete organic fertilizer mix from your garden center and use as recommended. Scratch fertilizers into the top 2 inches of vegetable gardens. For perennial gardens, don't dig at all. Spread fertilizers and lime, when needed, around the plants, water lightly, and cover with mulch.

6. Don't Forget The Nitrogen

Of all the essential plant nutrients, nitrogen deserves special mention. Though a living soil will continue to recycle and retain most other mineral nutrients, nitrogen is often in short supply, even after years of soil building. Not only does nitrogen feed soil plants, it also feeds soil organisms. Because of this, garden growth and long-term soil health depend on nitrogen.

Before planting every year, ensure sufficient nitrogen by counting all the sources you've added. Organic fertilizers, such as blood, seed, or feather meal, are sources of concentrated nitrogen. Fall or spring legume cover crops transfer nitrogen from the atmosphere to the soil. Manures or green grass clippings, incorporated as amendments, provide nitrogen as well. Compost, on the other hand, does not supply enough garden nitrogen. While compost is great for improving overall soil health, additional nitrogen sources are needed when using compost as an amendment.

7. Pull, Cover, Smother

As our garden wakes up in spring, so do the weeds. Before planting, get them under control. Weeds compete with garden plants, and from a soil perspective, they steal organic food away from the living soil.

For starters, fall mulching gives you the upper hand on spring weeds. Pull weeds that do emerge in the spring early and quickly, when they are small and easy to manage. If not noxious–that is, not spreading vigorously by root or stem–I suggest laying them right back on the soil surface and covering them with from 2 to 4 inches of organic mulch. Covering garden beds right from the start gives you the jump on garden weeds, while feeding the soil with organic material at the same time.

8. Recycle Perennials

If you have a landscape garden, hedges, woodlands, or fruit trees, then you have a wealth of materials to amend soils. Winter and early spring tree prunings, hedge trimmings, and perennial cuttings can feed the soil when recycled back into the garden.

Chipped yard debris and bits pruned from trees make effective mulch. When green, they also provide a valuable nitrogen source as a sheet mulch layer. Use softer perennial cuttings as mulch, sheet mulch compost, or a garden bed amendment. I like a natural look in my landscape gardens. I'll actually chop cuttings into smaller pieces and mulch them right below the perennials I've cut. This type of composting in place mimics the way plant litter falls in nature.

9. Let Soils Dry

For soils, it's often what we don't do, as much as what we do, that matters. Before planting spring gardens, the most important soil care priority is letting wet spring soils dry. Digging, walking on, or driving a rototiller over wet soils, particularly those with clays, compacts and damages the soil structure we work so hard to build. When this happens, we literally squeeze the air out of soils, leaving little space for organisms to breathe or roots to grow.

To tell when your soils are ready to work in the spring, take a handful and squeeze. If water comes out, hold off for a week or so. Soils that form a sturdy ball when molded or clay soils that press into a shiny ribbon also need to dry more.

The Definitive Guide to Building Deep Rich Soils by Imitating Nature

As some of you may have heard, I've finally got my hands on a piece of a land and now when I'm finally able to get my hands dirty I'm faced with the reality of my shallow, compacted, alkaline and sometimes waterlogged for months soils. This has come as a huge disappointment as I had big plans for annual gardens, food forests and perennial grasslands.

After taking a deeper look into this subject, I began to realize that, in essence, my only two options are importing good soil (not going to happen!) or improving the soil I already have. The latter offers me the chance to regenerate the soils and actually learn something about soil and soil biology, so I've now embraced the challenge.

Something fascinating I learnt while reading up on the subject is that there are more microorganisms in a teaspoon full of healthy soil than there are people in the world. When we add in earthworms, nematodes and other soil life we can see that there is much more to soil than we realize looking down from above.

This kind of biological richness is something that we in permaculture should try to replicate in our gardens. But what I've learned is that emulating a grassland is different than emulating a forest, and for this reason you first have to be clear on which ecosystem you're trying to copy. Here is why.

Ecological succession as a model for improving the soil

Ecological succession is a process of change in the species structure over time. The established species influence the soil composition and alter it over time. As you can see from my sketches there is a significant difference in soil found in the bare field than in the forest. The main difference lies in what kind of microbes are most prevalent in the soil and what they feed upon. Generally, fungi respond to surface decomposition, whereas bacteria prefer soil disturbance.

The weight of fungi present in forest soils is much greater than the weight of bacteria. In grasslands, however, there is around an equal distribution of the two. In agricultural soils that are routinely tilled, in contrast, the weight of fungi is less than that of bacteria.

But how does this apply to me, you may ask? Well, if you are trying to create a healthy pasture or self-fertilizing food forest, or even just a productive annual garden you will need to simulate the conditions where the intended plants are originally found.

So, let's look at three most common situations you'll be faced with on your farm: annual gardens, grasslands and food forests, and see what steps you can take to bring your soil to life.

1. Annual Gardens/Market Gardens

Annual plants colonize bare soil following a disturbance. As they wither and die at the end of their growing season their remains fall on the ground and act as mulch that bacteria and earthworms feed upon. This cycle repeats itself annually, with organic matter building and the creation of humus. Here is what to do to replicate these conditions.

Don't disturb the subsoil and encourage biological tillage

As can be seen in nature, to establish annuals you have to intervene mechanically to prepare beds for crop planting and establishment. However, you don't want till deep as you don't want to disturb the soil structure.

The undisturbed subsoil lets earthworms dig their tunnels and provides aeration and drainage while their exertions bind together crumbs of soil. They play an important role in healthy soil structure and replace mechanical with biological tillage.

If you don't compromise earthworms, microbes and other soil organisms through soil inversion they can perform much of the tillage needed to create and maintain loose, fertile soils. However, if your soils are biologically dead those microbes have to come from somewhere and that is why we are sometimes required to feed the soil with already biologically-active decomposed organic matter rich in beneficial microbes – the compost

Bring your soil to life with compost

Good compost supplies both the organic matter for soil building and the fertilizer for the crops, and, most importantly, it's packed with soil organisms that trigger biological activity. It inoculates your soil with microbes that will digest nutrients present in the soil and feed your plants.

Compost is the key ingredient for building and maintaining healthy soil. Because of its special characteristics, compost cannot simply be replaced with manure, natural fertilizers or green manure.If you've just moved to a new garden and want productivity, then compost will rapidly make your soils fertile.

Maintain organic matter with mulch

Once you have your soil biology working for you, you need to feed it so it can feed your plants.There are a number of different ways to maintain soil organic matter in your annual garden. One of the easiest is using lawn grass clippings, leaves, straw or cover crops and, of course, compost.

The mulch is then left on the surface to decompose. Adding this layer of organic matter and spreading it is, in effect, 'composting in place', where the garden beds become large composting areas. Then by the actions of earthworms, bacteria, fungi and insects, the organic matter is slowly broken down and released into the soil, providing nutrients to the garden.

While all this sounds great if you are running a market garden operation, this kind of practice is restrictive and somewhat impractical. Here is what JM Fortier in his book The Market Gardener has to say: "Based on my experience, direct seeding into crop residues, mulch, or crimped down cover crops is not straightforward, causing unpredictable germination rates – a nightmare for any commercial grower." Something we should bear in mind.

Use crop rotation to mimic diversity

With crop rotation you can actually mimic the diversity of annual plants growing on a bare field. Differing root systems among plants penetrate the soil to different depths, improving its structure.

By ensuring crop diversity and alternating crops you allow soil to keep producing without being drained of its nutrients, while simultaneously eliminating a number of diseases and harmful insects that often occur when one species is continuously cropped.

2. Grasslands – Pasture/Cropland

As we move in succession the perennial grasses are slowly taking over. Big herbivores are roaming in herds feeding off these grasses, trampling them down and fertilizing the soils. Over long periods of time organic matter simply built up and now we have fungi and mycelium with bacteria, equally represented.

Don't disturb the soil – ensure the lowest level of mechanical disturbance possible

Unless you need to repair the compacted soil, poor drainage or have to do some initial tillage to sow the perennial cover, you should aim for no till, no compaction and lowest possible mechanical disturbance. Make your tillage minimal.

Here the goal is the same as with an annual garden, enabling the biological tillage but also taking advantage of the mycorrhizal fungi which form symbiotic relationships with the roots, extending the plant's root network. They also prevent pathogens, improve water use efficiency and the efficiency of absorbing other nutrients.

Always keep your soil covered with perennial cover crops

If we look at perennial native ranges we can see they are permanently covered. So the first step to rebuilding soil structure and health of a grassland is to get it under perennial cover. This acts like armor for the soil. Bare soil is detrimental to its health, you only find bare soil in catastrophic events or where humans have imposed their will upon it.

Cover crops are planted specifically to build and hold soil and to smother weeds. They range from long-growing perennials to short-term green manures but the aim is the same: a solid cover of plants. Their leaves will protect the soil from hammering rains and eventually their residue carpets the surface with nutritious, humus-building matter.

Plant diverse perennial cover crops

Once again, if you look at native perennial ecosystems we can see diversity. Rather than resorting to one or two species of cover crops they should be seeded as multi-species combinations, through doing so, you are mimicking what nature does. You optimize solar energy collection as different plants have different shaped leaves. Because the roots penetrate to varying depths the mycorrhizal fungi are able to deliver moisture and nutrients from the different areas of the soil profile.

You can design your cover crops to address whatever specific concerns you may wish: whether it's protection of the soil as living mulches, adding organic matter as green manure, boosting fertility with N fixing legumes or dealing with compaction. Even if you are using your grassland for growing cash crops, you can maximize your profits by mixing in cover crops. Cover crops can be sown before, with, or after the cash crop. This way you have something growing all the time.

Planned disturbance in a form of animal impact and planned grazing

In nature soils are formed in conjunction with herbivores. In this case through large herds of herbivores moving across the planes, but also by other local wildlife; rabbits, grasshoppers, and other insects. All of them are taking this forage, the biomass, and endlessly recycling it.

Animals are an integral part of a healthy ecosystem. But how can they help you to build healthy soil?

A prime example of building soil with big herbivores is the holistic planned grazing practice conducted by Allan Savory and others like Greg Judy. They use high-density animal herds that graze a paddock for one day before being moved to the next paddock. Joel Salatin has a similar technique, he has a grazing plan with a high-density herd impact followed by ample recovery time.

The goal is for animals to consume a third of the grass in the paddock and trample the rest into the soil to feed earthworms and soil microbes, thus replicating the natural herds of large grazers that coevolved with grasses.

3. Food Forests/Permaculture Orchards

With time every ecosystem will eventually end up forest-like. In a forest, organic matter in the form of fallen leaves, twigs and branches and dying plants, are all deposited on the forest floor, where they are decomposed into rich humus by the action of fungi and other organisms. Fungal fabrics, mycelium run through the top few inches and act as interfaces between plant roots and nutrients, bringing distant nutrients and moisture to the host plant, extending the absorption zone well beyond the root structure. No tree could reach maturity without this symbiotic relationship.

Food forests are actually younger versions of the mature forests, in his book Creating Forest Gardens Martin Crawford explains- "A food forest is a forest modelled on the structure of young natural woodland and it often contains nitrogen-fixing trees and shrubs, which are pioneer species, establishing quickly and improving soil and environmental conditions for other trees to follow."

If you are starting from scratch let's see how you can transform bare land to a food forest.

Improve your soil with green manures and transitional ground-covers

Preparing the soil prior to planting offers certain advantages. A year of cover cropping and woody mulching not only offers a chance to build organic matter and correct fertility imbalances but, most importantly, accelerates fungal dominance. Fruit trees generally prefer high-quality soil and that's why it is particularly important to achieve a good layer of humus and to try to use as much biomass as possible on the soil.

Following the initial tillage or sheet mulching, existing grasses will generally be ready for cover crops, preferably red or crimson clover as these two nitrogen-fixing legumes have a stronger affinity for mycorrhizal fungi. Other Legumes and dynamic accumulator plants are also acceptable, and all of these can be even oversown into existing grasses.

Inoculate your soil with mycorrhizal fungi

Food Forest soils ideally contain a fungal presence ten times higher than that of bacteria. If you're starting with bare field and there are no fungi present you can encourage mycorrhizal associations through inoculation with fungi. Here is what Michael Crawford recommends in his book Creating Forest Gardens:

Dip exposed roots of seedlings into water enriched with the spore mass of one or more mycorrhizal species.

Broadcast spores onto the root zones of existing trees and shrubs, using spores in a water carrier.

Place a little soil from the root zone of proven mushroom-producing trees around seedlings, either in the nursery or soon after planting.

Inoculate the compost of pot-grown plants with a mixture of dried spores from suitable species.

When planting trees or shrubs, scatter a dry spore mixture into the planting hole.

Use woody mulch to feed the fungi

Compost, deciduous wood chips, and other woody material can be added on top of the green manure crops. The woody material is what drives the fungal dominance you want for a healthy food forest. The goal, plain and simple, is to create what Michael Phillips in Holistic Orchard calls fungal duff – the litter layer where mineralization and humification take place through the action of fungi.

Mulching with wood chips and chopping and dropping woody plant material on the ground helps mycorrhizae thrive, and it's this fungal connection that provides the balanced nutrition necessary for a tree to better withstand disease.

Create self-sustaining fertility with nitrogen fixing trees and dynamic accumulator plants

The self-fertilising nature of the food forest comes from the use of nitrogen-fixing plants along with other plants like comfrey that are particularly good at raising nutrients from the subsoil. Through their use efficient nutrient cycling develops in a forest-like system, maximizing fertility for other plants to grow.

Nitrogen fixers are extremely useful fertility providers in a food forest. Techniques like 'chop and drop' mulches, coppicing and pollarding from these plants in particular can release the nutrients they have extracted over time from the earth or air. Simply having them shed leaves on the ground can improve fertility.

Building Healthy Soil

Though some gardeners may be blessed with perfect soil, most of us garden in soil that is less than perfect. If your soil has too much clay in it, is too sandy, too stony or too acidic, don't despair. Turning a poor soil into a plant-friendly soil is not difficult to do, once you understand the components of a healthy soil.

Soil is composed of weathered rock and organic matter, water and air. But the hidden "magic" in a healthy soil is the organisms—small animals, worms, insects and microbes—that flourish when the other soil elements are in balance.

Minerals. Roughly half of the soil in your garden consists of small bits of weathered rock that has gradually been broken down by the forces of wind, rain, freezing and thawing and other chemical and biological processes.

Soil type is generally classified by the size of these inorganic soil particles: sand (large particles), silt (medium-sized particles) or clay (very small particles). The proportion of sand, silt and clay particles determines the texture of your soil and affects drainage and nutrient availability, which in turn influence how well your plants will grow.

Organic Matter. Organic matter is the partially decomposed remains of soil organisms and plant life including lichens and mosses, grasses and leaves, trees, and all other kinds of vegetative matter.

Although it only makes up a small fraction of the soil (normally 5 to 10 percent), organic matter is absolutely essential. It binds together soil particles into porous crumbs or granules which allow air and water to move through the soil. Organic matter also retains moisture (humus holds up to 90 percent of its weight in water), and is able to absorb and store nutrients. Most importantly, organic matter is food for microorganisms and other forms of soil life.

You can increase the amount of organic matter in your soil by adding compost, aged animal manures, green manures (cover crops), mulches or peat moss. Because most soil life and plant roots are located in the top 6 inches of soil, concentrate on this upper layer. To learn more about making your own compost, read All About Composting.

Be cautious about incorporating large amounts of high-carbon material (straw, leaves, wood chips and sawdust). Soil microorganisms will consume a lot of nitrogen in their efforts to digest these materials and they may deprive your plants of nitrogen in the short run.

Soil life. Soil organisms include the bacteria and fungi, protozoa and nematodes, mites, springtails, earthworms and other tiny creatures found in healthy soil. These organisms are essential for plant growth. They help convert organic matter and soil minerals into the vitamins, hormones, disease-suppressing compounds and nutrients that plants need to grow.

Their excretions also help to bind soil particles into the small aggregates that make a soil loose and crumbly. As a gardener, your job is to create the ideal conditions for these soil organisms to do their work. This means providing them with an abundant source of food (the carbohydrates in organic matter), oxygen (present in a well-aerated soil), and water (an adequate but not excessive amount).

Air. A healthy soil is about 25 percent air. Insects microbes, earthworms and soil life require this much air to live. The air in soil is also an important source of the atmospheric nitrogen that is utilized by plants.

Well-aerated soil has plenty of pore space between the soil particles or crumbs. Fine soil particles (clay or silt) have tiny spaces between them - in some cases too small for air to penetrate. Soil composed of large particles, like sand, has large pore spaces and contains plenty of air. But, too much air can cause organic matter to decompose too quickly.

To ensure that there is a balanced supply of air in your soil, add plenty of organic matter, avoid stepping in the growing beds or compacting the soil with heavy equipment and never work the soil when it is very wet.

Water. A healthy soil will also contain about 25 percent water. Water, like air, is held in the pore spaces between soil particles. Large pore spaces allow rain and irrigation water to move down to the root zone and into the subsoil. In sandy soils, the spaces between the soil particles are so large that gravity causes water to drain down and out very quickly. That's why sandy soils dry out so fast.

Small pore spaces permit water to migrate back upwards through the process of capillary action. In waterlogged soils, water has completely filled the pore spaces, forcing out all the air. This suffocates soil organisms as well as plant roots.

Ideally, your soil should have a combination of large and small pore spaces. Again, organic matter is the key, because it encourages the formation of aggregate, or crumbs, or soil. Organic matter also absorbs water and retains it until it is needed by plant roots.

Every soil has a different combination of these five basic components. By balancing them you can dramatically improve your soil's healthy and your garden's productivity. But first, you need to know what kind of soil you have.

Soil Texture and Type

Soil texture can range from very fine particles to coarse and gravelly. You don't have to be a scientist to determine the texture of the soil in your garden. To get a rough idea, simply place some soil in the palm of your hand and wet it slightly, then run the mixture between your fingers. If it feels gritty, your soil is sandy; if it feels smooth, like moist talcum powder, your soil is silty; if it feels harsh when dry, sticky or slippery when wet, or rubbery when moist, it is high in clay.

Every soil has unique physical characteristics, which are determined by how it was formed. The silty soil found in an old floodplain is inherently different from stony mountain soil; the clay soil that lay under a glacier for millions of years is unlike the sandy soil near an ocean. Some of these basic qualities can be improved with proper management—or made worse by abuse.

Identifying your soil type: Soils are generally described according to the predominant type of soil particle present: sand, silt or clay. By conducting a simple soil test, you can easily see what kind of soil you're dealing with. You may want to repeat this test with several different soil samples from your lawn and garden.

1. Fill a quart jar about one-third full with topsoil and add water until the jar is almost full.

2. Screw on the lid and shake the mixture vigorously, until all the clumps of soil have dissolved.

3. Now set the jar on a windowsill and watch as the larger particles begin to sink to the bottom.

4. In a minute or two the sand portion of the soil will have settled to the bottom of the jar. Mark the level of sand on the side of the jar.

5. Leave the jar undisturbed for several hours. The finer silt particles will gradually settle onto the sand. You will find the layers are slightly different colors, indicating various types of particles.

6. Leave the jar overnight. The next layer above the silt will be clay. Mark the thickness of that layer. On top of the clay will be a thin layer of organic matter. Some of this organic matter may still be floating in the water. In fact, the jar should be murky and full of floating organic sediments. If not, you probably need to add organic matter to improve the soil's fertility and structure.

Improving Soil Structure

Even very poor soil can be dramatically improved, and your efforts will be well rewarded. With their roots in healthy soil, your plants will be more vigorous and more productive.

Sandy Soil. Sand particles are large, irregularly shaped bits of rock. In a sandy soil, large air spaces between the sand particles allow water to drain very quickly. Nutrients tend to drain away with the water, often before plants have a chance to absorb them. For this reason, sandy soils are usually nutrient-poor.

A sandy soil also has so much air in it that microbes consume organic matter very quickly. Because sandy soils usually contain very little clay or organic matter, they don't have much of a crumb structure. The soil particles don't stick together, even when they're wet.

To improve sandy soil:

- Work in 3 to 4 inches of organic matter such as well-rotted manure or finished compost.

- Mulch around your plants with leaves, wood chips, bark, hay or straw. Mulch retains moisture and cools the soil.

- Add at least 2 inches of organic matter each year.

- Grow cover crops or green manures.

Clay Soil. Clay particles are small and flat. They tend to pack together so tightly that there is hardly any pore space at all. When clay soils are wet, they are sticky and practically unworkable. They drain slowly and can stay waterlogged well into the spring. Once they finally dry out, they often become hard and cloddy, and the surface cracks into flat plates.

Lack of pore space means that clay soils are generally low in both organic matter and microbial activity. Plant roots are stunted because it is too hard for them to push their way through the soil. Foot traffic and garden equipment can cause compaction problems. Fortunately, most clay soils are rich in minerals which will become available to your plants once you improve the texture of the soil.

To improve clay soil:

- Work 2 to 3 inches of organic matter into the surface of the soil. Then add at least 1 inch more each year after that.
- Add the organic matter in the fall, if possible.
- Use permanent raised beds to improve drainage and keep foot traffic out of the growing area.
- Minimize tilling and spading.

Silty Soil. Silty soils contain small irregularly shaped particles of weathered rock, which means they are usually quite dense and have relatively small pore spaces and poor drainage. They tend to be more fertile than either sandy or clayey soils.

To improve silty soil:

- Add at least 1 inch of organic matter each year.
- Concentrate on the top few inches of soil to avoid surface crusting.
- Avoid soil compaction by avoiding unnecessary tilling and walking on garden beds.
- Consider constructing raised beds.

Soil pH

The pH level of your soil indicates its relative acidity or alkalinity. A pH test measures the ratio of hydrogen (positive) ions to hydroxyl (negative) ions in the soil water. When hydrogen and hydroxyl ions are present in equal amounts, the pH is said to be neutral (pH 7). When the hydrogen ions prevail, the soil is acidic (pH 1 to pH 6.5). And when the hydroxyl ions tip the balance, the pH is alkaline (pH 6.8 to pH 14).

Most essential plant nutrients are soluble at pH levels of 6.5 to 6.8, which is why most plants grow best in this range. If the pH of your soil is much higher or lower, soil nutrients start to become chemically bound to the soil particles, which makes them unavailable to your plants. Plant health suffers because the roots are unable to absorb the nutrients they require.

To improve the fertility of your soil, you need to get the pH of your soil within the 6.5 to 6.8 range. You can't, and shouldn't try, to change the pH of your soil overnight. Instead, gradually alter it over one or two growing seasons and then maintain it every year thereafter. Liberal applications of organic matter is a good idea too, because it helps to moderate pH imbalances.

Acidic Soil. If the pH of your soil is less than 6.5, it may be too acidic for most garden plants (although some, such as blueberries and azaleas require acidic soil). Soils in the eastern half of the U.S. are usually on the acidic side.

The most common way to raise the pH of your soil (make it less acidic) is to add powdered limestone.

Dolomitic limestone will also add manganese to the soil. Apply it in the fall because it takes several months to alter the pH.

Wood ash will also raise the pH, and it works more quickly than limestone and contains potassium and trace elements. But if you add too much wood ash, you can drastically alter the pH and cause nutrient imbalances. For best results, apply wood ash in the winter, and apply no more than 2 pounds per 100 square feet, every two to three years.

To raise the pH of your soil by about one point:

- In sandy soil: add 3 to 4 pounds of ground limestone per 100 square feet.
- In loam (good garden soil): add 7 to 8 pounds per 100 square feet.
- In heavy clay: add 8 to 10 pounds per 100 square feet.
- Alkaline Soil. If your soil is higher than 6.8, you will need to acidify your soil. Soils in the western

U.S., especially in arid regions, are typically alkaline. Soil is usually acidified by adding ground sulfur. You can also incorporate naturally acidic organic materials such as conifer needles, sawdust, peat moss and oak leaves.

To lower soil pH by about one point:

- In sandy soil: add 1 pound ground sulphur per 100 square feet.
- In loam (good garden soil): add 1.5 to 2 pounds per 100 square feet.
- In heavy clay: add 2 pounds per 100 square feet.

Soil Testing

A professional soil test will provide you with a wealth of information about your soil, including the pH and amount of different nutrients.

Your local Cooperative Extension Service office may offer a professional soil testing service. The advantage is low cost and results that are specifically geared to your location. If this service is not available, you can also have your soil tested by an independent soil lab. If possible, choose one in your own region of the country.

Soil test results usually rate the levels of soil pH, phosphorus, potassium, magnesium, calcium, and sometimes nitrogen. (Most labs do not test for nitrogen because it is so unstable in the soil.) Some labs also offer tests for micronutrients such as boron, zinc and manganese. Unless you feel there may be a deficiency problem, you probably won't need micronutrient testing. As a preventative measure, you can apply organic fertilizers that include micronutrients (such as greensand and kelp meal).

To get the most accurate test results, take a soil sample from each garden area: lawn, flower garden, and vegetable garden. Spring and fall are the best times to perform a soil test. The soil is more stable, and these are good times to incorporate any recommended fertilizers.

Many labs will give recommendations for specific organic amendments upon request. If not, you will have to compare labels to find organic substitutes for the chemical fertilizers that may be suggested.

Conclusion

With each of the scenarios outlined above you are striving for the highest percent of organic matter in your soil and providing habitats for a high diversity of soil food web organisms. In an annual garden this would be geared more towards bacteria and in a forest garden more towards mycorrhizal fungi.

The easiest way to know what your plants need is to ask yourself: "Where did the plant grow natively, Field or Forest?

Depending on the type of system you wish to achieve, bring animals into the system in any way you can. They help with organic matter and nutrient cycling:

earthworms, herbivores, poultry, all are integral to system health.

And always remember nature is our greatest teacher, working in harmony with nature is always the best way to proceed, so whatever you're planning to do always ask yourself: "What would nature do, how would this system I'm trying to set-up look naturally? And then adapt it to your circumstances.